William James McClure

Poems

William James McClure

Poems

ISBN/EAN: 9783741112713

Manufactured in Europe, USA, Canada, Australia, Japa

Cover: Foto ©Andreas Hilbeck / pixelio.de

Manufactured and distributed by brebook publishing software (www.brebook.com)

William James McClure

Poems

POEMS.

BY

WILLIAM JAMES McCLURE.

NEW YORK:
P. O'SHEA, PUBLISHER, 27 BARCLAY STREET.

1869.

Entered according to Act of Congress, in the year 1869,
By WILLIAM JAMES McCLURE,
In the Clerk's Office of the District Court of the United States for the
Southern District of New York.

ALVORD, PRINTER.

Dedicated

TO THE

POETIC GENIUS

OF

AMERICA.

PREFACE.

With these Poems as my credentials, I knock at the garden-gate of Poesy. Content to enter the dales, but aspiring to the hills of Song, I pray ye, tuneful Sisters, favor my lyre, and let me in!

From the Literary World I ask a just and candid criticism; and if there be found aught in this volume elevating to the mind, or touching to the heart of Humanity, I shall not regret the labor of its production.

To the friends who have encouraged and assisted me in my authorship I tender undying thanks.

Regardful of approval, and respecting censure, when proceeding from competent judgment, I present my first book to the public.

W. J. McC.

New York, February 1, 1869.

CONTENTS.

	PAGE
ZILLORA, A TALE, IN THREE CANTOS	9

GATHERINGS OF SONG.

I.

✓ THE HUDSON RIVER	52
✓ MOONLIGHT ON THE HUDSON	57
NATIVE HILLS	59
THE WOODLAND BRIDGE	61
BUDS AND BLOSSOMS	63
A WAIF	66
SUMMER	67
VIOLETS AND PANSIES	69
MORNING—GLORIES	71
SONG OF THE MOWERS	73
AUTUMN	75

	PAGE
OCTOBER	77
THE FALL OF THE LEAVES	79
WINTER'S VICTIM	80

II.

SWEET IS THE SONG	83
BEAUTY	84
FRIENDSHIP	85
MEETING AND PARTING	86
LA SEÑORITA	89
ON THE LAKE	91
AFFECTION FOR NATURE	93
A SKETCH	94
THE PURE AND THE LOVELY	95
MY BEAUTIFUL ANGEL	97
MARY	99

III.

WAR	100
BATTLE OF LOOKOUT MOUNTAIN	102
GLIMPSES	106
TO THE ANGEL, PEACE	109
EXULTATION	111
COUNSEL	113
PRAISE	115
THE SHAMROCK AND LAUREL	116

CONTENTS.

	PAGE
✓ The Rights of Man	118
✓ Thomas Francis Meagher	120
✓ The Memory of the Brave	122

IV.

Nature and Art	124
Society's Sea	128
A Vision	131
To Tragedy	133
The Outcast's Grave	134
Wealth no Merit	136
Changes	138
Morality	140
Remember Death	141
Lines to a Brilliant Star	143
An Impression	144
Stanzas	146
✓ The New Year	147
Ambition	148

ZILLORA.

A TALE.

CANTO FIRST.

BRIGHT MUSE, of upward wing!
Wilt thou light me to sing
Of mystic spirit-realms—
Where cypresses and elms
Have not a germ, nor tears
The boon of lovely eyes?—
Or of the hopes and fears,
The laughter and the sighs
Of human hearts?—Speak, and advise!

And thus the Muse: O sing
Of Love's sweet wakening;
Its growth and riper hours,
When o'er its life come showers,
To chasten and refresh
The rankness of its bloom!
'Twill ne'er decay, as flesh
Within the clod-claspt tomb—
A child of Heaven, 'twill Heaven resume.

Earth, fondled by the Sea,
Avowed its grief and glee,
In sprightly tones and deep—
As though the genii 'd keep
Their moanings heard, 'midst strains
Of fairy mirth and smiles—
Vibrating to the plains,
The crags and dim defiles,
That form and guard the Grecian isles.

Greece of Old! Poesy's
Sublimest galleries
Are rich with scenes of thine;
For thou'rt the poet's shrine:
The spirit of Homer's
Thought pervades thy valleys,
Heights, and waters; roamers—
Like he who, charmed, dallies—
On thee gaze rapt, and as rallies

Mem'ry her noiseless train,
The bosom flames, the brain
Lightens, the soul acquires
Song from a thousand lyres!—
How kingly was thy Past,
Classic land: thy Present—
How into thralldom cast.
Grand and finely pleasant,
Slave thou art 'twixt Cross and Crescent.

Survive methinks in thee
The heart-throbs of the Free!
Thy regeneration—
Oh, that it were but won!
Behold heroic Crete—
Her war-flag streams the sky,[1]
Her valor spurns defeat:
Oh, may the rude Turk fly
Her coasts, or thereon vanquished die!

The sun's last beam with red
Tinged the summer-clouds, wed
To grandeur-gifted days;
And, as anon its blaze
Sank less lurid beneath
Mediterranean's wave,
There floated on the breath
Of zephyrs sounds that brave
Men wish to hear, and monarchs crave.

In the dreamy twilight,
Rock-browed stood height on height,
Hollowed by dizz'ning chasms,
In which the thund'rous spasms
Of cataracts were heard—
Terrific and unsipt;
And "Good-night"—kindly word—
By civil voices lipt,
Heralded repose, slumber-dipt.

Awful Spirit of Night!
Thy lone and solemn flight
Enforces deepest thought,
And meditation fraught
With fantasies and dreams.
Thy wings the land and wave
O'erspread, concealing beams—
Save when, through Heaven's concave,
The moon and stars thy shadows brave.

The poet cons his verse,
The worldling counts his purse;
The lover wildly vows,
His mistress to espouse;
The outcast by-lanes roves,
The debauchee insane
Through Pleasure's orgies moves—
A demon in his brain—
While thou, O Night, o'er earth remain.

To children's eyelids comes
Soft sleep, pervading homes
Of Poverty and Wealth.
Lovingly and by stealth,
Each mother kisses each
Young flower, then wooes repose;
Ere which her prayers beseech
God's sunshine on her rose,
Whose bud new-opes, unwise of snows!

Dimly and moonlight-kissed,
Ruins loomed—power-dismissed,
 Yet haughty still—their crests
Stubborn to Time's unrests;
For o'er them javelins glowed,
And helmets proud, in days
When mailed warriors strode
The halls—high, curving ways—
And women's eyes lent laughing rays.

Oh, splendors that the mind
And hand of man designed,
And palpably upreared!—
Why are ye so endeared,
E'en in your sad decay?
True monuments! ye stand
Weird warners by the way;
And dignify the land
With recollections, martial, bland.

Huge on a cliff appeared
A castle, old and seared,
Whose battlements all bore
The signature of war,
That reddened simpler ages;
And standing 'bove the sea,
Calmly brooked its rages—
As views Humanity
A fierce beast caged, though littered free!

Lights flashed from porticoes:
Again, again arose
Glad music's tone; anon
'Twould cease, as though 'twere gone,
Then sound again, and charm.
There merry-moving feet
Tript blithe, and arm pressed arm
Of dear companion sweet—
Consorting loves and friendships meet.

Mirth came in gracious glees
From broad-arched entrances;
For Pleasure, high-enthroned,
Made Grief's voice undertoned;
And firmamental gems—
That deck th' ethereal round,
And kindle theorems
In human minds profound—
Sparkled o'er horizontal bound.

One year a bride that day—
That eve 'twere right to say—
Zillora welcome gave
To hearts from o'er the wave;
Yet wished that silence filled,
Instead of revelry,
Her dome of warlike build—
Where ancient devilry
Recorded was as chivalry!

Courtiers, fostering style,
And lady-peers, the while
Entered the castle-hall:
Its ev'ry arch and wall,
And columned gallery,
Festooned with artist-taste:
Honoring socially
Zillora's wifehood chaste—
Vivanco's station, legend-traced.

It was a festive eve,
And Beauty chose to weave
With Joy concurrent charms.
All thoughtless of alarms,
The gay assemblage danced
The corridors along—
Sculptured and mirror-tranced.
Not sinless was the throng,
For gilding oft conceals a wrong.

Zillora pensively
Reclined 'midst tapestry.
A looker-on, she was
A shrinker from applause
And gayety—to thought
Disposed—most nobly fair;
Clothed in fine fabrics, wrought
Where to the cloudless air
Melts incense, worship to declare

There glistened o'er her brow,
And on her breast below,
Jewels from India's mines—
Brighter than brightest wines,
Or sunlit waterfalls,
Emitting crystal sprays!—
Befitting Fashion's halls,
Where envious beauties gaze,
And long for follies till they craze!

Her robes of showy worth
Accorded with the mirth
Of all her laughing guests,
Not with her heart's behests;
For 'twas on such an eve,
But not from such a scene,
Young Love lured her to leave
Her cottage, tricked in green,
Round which she roved, a crownless queen.

As thus Zillora mused,
Her tresses dark refused
Art-pinioning, and lay
In Nature's untaught way
Upon her neck, and down
Unto her bodice rolled,
In waves of glossy brown;
Unheeding frill and fold
Of her attire, inweaved with gold.

ZILLORA.

Vivanco hovered near,
His healthful visage clear
Turned from the guests away.
Ere long a sudden ray
Vivacious 'thwart his face
Would gleam; and while its glare
His spirit held, the place,
And those assembled there,
Of joy partook a double share.

He loved his beauteous wife:
Zillora's gentle life
Was dearer to his soul
Than richest earth-control.
And he had wide domains
Of meadow-land and shore—
Compounded were his gains—
Trim ships him treasure bore—
He was an island governor.

Light-tonnaged trading-fleets
Were his resource; their feats
The Levant knew; the Nile
They entered oft, and while
This merchant-grandee slept,
His cargoes from their decks
In lieu of coin were swept.
What marvel, then, that wrecks
Vivanco's dreams should often vex.

His was a tropic blood,
And flushed his veins for good—
As rivulets the land
Traverse, and bloom expand;
For withering evil,
When fell revenge impelled
Diversion to the devil—
Like stormy waves, unheld
By human art, by Nature quelled.

But to the theme.—The dance
Survived, and Music's lance,
Rapture-tipt, pierced each heart,
Striking the kindliest part,
Chasing the heaviness
That often drags lives down
To brooding and distress—
The product of a frown,
Or consciousness of friendships flown.

Stilled at last was the beat
Of instruments and feet:
The sea's incessant call
Told not of festival;
Yet its waves from the stars
Obtained a brilliancy,
Till their crests seemed like cars
That in fairy-land be—
Silverly-adorned, vapory.

The turret-headed towers,
Buttressed to stony powers,
Were spectral in the gleam
Of the moon's modest beam:
That wandered with the light
Of festive lamps and brief,
Far, far into the night—
As roams a kingly chief
With one who holds a lesser fief!

Excitement waned, grew cold;
Some rested, others strolled,
And fanned their throbbing brows:
Belike betrothment vows
Were given, and promise
Of a future meeting:
Surely there shone a bliss
In each eye competing—
Seen through glances, love-entreating.

Voice-vivified, arose
Zillora's song; as flows
A spring-brook down a dell,
In murm'rous music, fell
Its cadences purely:
Through the hushed castle chimed—
Not sadly, demurely,
But trustful,—its tones, timed
To yearning heart-thoughts, love-sublimed.

1.

There flew a little bird to me,
    It nestled in my virgin breast;
I could not tell it to be free,
    'Twas in its gentle thrall so blest—
'Twas in its gentle thrall so blest,
    So joyous with supernal glee,
That it would seek no other nest,
    In grove, or vale, or summer lea.

2.

It came unseen, 'twas all my own;
    It sang so heavenly day by day,
That ev'ry thought took up its tone,
    And mused no more the roundelay—
And mused no more the roundelay
    Of wilds and waters, bloom-o'ergrown;
Borne by a mystic power away
    To dreams of light and joy unknown.

3.

Methinks my little minstrel flew,
    A cherub, from the highest sky;
So unlamenting and so true,
    If 'twere to die I too would die—
If 'twere to die I too would die,
    And soar the heavens beyond the blue:
My heart should then have lost the tie,
    That binds me, husband, unto you!

Among the arches strong,
Zillora's tender song
Faint echoed, and then died.
Hilarity replied,
Upswelling from the strand,
Where blithesome forms had met
To rove the moonlit land,
Or foot the minuet
To gypsy-lute and flageolet.

List to the merry din
Of strollers coming in;
List to the banquet-sound,
As coteries surround,
And Hospitality
Its bounteousness outpours.
Behold the livery—
The gilding on the doors—
The shadows on the walls and floors!

Glasses clinked; 'twas in truth
A scene of Mirth and Youth.
Meats and fruits the sideboards
Filled, and jellied hoards
Enticed the luscious taste
Of swain and sweet-mouthed maid.
Nor was there aught of haste:
Long, long the feast delayed,
And wine and wit in wassail played.

"Adieu" was said, until
"Adieu" said all, and still
The zephyrs breathed "adieu,"
And up their currents flew,
As gallant vessels plied
Toward their havens near;
Bearing with white wings wide
Concordant spirits dear—
True elements of social cheer.

Vivanco's castle stark,
High in the deep'ning dark,
Reared rayless as the stone
Whereon its base was thrown.
No sylphic dance, no feast,
No music to invite:
The moon had quit the East,
The moon had quit the Night,
And Peace grew solemn—weary quite.

ZILLORA.

CANTO SECOND.

BEAUTIFUL MORN! the hills
Resumed thy luster; rills,
Like myriad-blended eyes,
Drew radiance from thy skies;
And manse and forest flowers,
Of many hues and forms,
Looked coyish from their bowers,
To bright blue heaven that warms,
Full innocent of hidden storms.

The Sea, the Land, and Man,—
Proud works that show the plan
Of High Omnipotence—
Evinced their thankful sense
For rays that earthward coursed:
Now meager as faint beams,
Through dungeon-crannies forced;
Then mantling hills and streams,
In matin-robes of merry gleams.

Oh, why should Grief survive
The Night, or if alive
When Joy o'er Nature comes,
Why lurks it in fair homes,
A torment-shade?—till Life
Implores in spirit-woe:
" Blest Heaven! undo this strife—

Sweet Saviour, let thy glow
Descend and soothe me, sad and low!"

However change the skies,
Emotions rest, and rise
To paroxysms the same—
As startling smoke and flame
From capitals outburst:
They flicker on the hearth,
Till roused by hand accurst;
Then blaze along the earth,
And Lamentation make of Mirth.

The peasant joined his toil,
The potentate of spoil
And Pleasure's mock'ries shared,
As brave Vivanco dared
The fretful, surging sea.
Zillora's close caress,
And prayer, ere parted he
The shore, raised Happiness
And Hope, nor made fond Love the less.

And oh! the picture given,
Of waters, ships, and Heaven;
Of mountains, distant, dull,
Yet misty-beautiful;
Of high, historic lands,

Honored by crumbling shrines,
And laved by streams, whose sands—
Revealing tide-declines—
Besprinkled seemed with diamond signs!

Mayhap on some green height
A maiden stood; her light
Garb flowing, and her hand
O'er her heart, as she scanned
Vivanco's vessels speed
The tossing tide along:
Her thoughts such thoughts that plead
When true Love feareth wrong—
Entranced in this plain passion-song:

1.

God guide those noble ships,
   Departing o'er the sea;
And keep from taint the manly lips,
   That told their love to me.

2.

Oh, youthful mariner,
   When distant beauty lures,
Be ever faithful unto her,
   Whose love for thee endures.

3.

My heart would sorrowed die,
   And I, a stricken thing,

Should hurry to Eternity,
  If thine prove varying!

4.

Adieu, O noble ships!
  May kind gales waft ye on,
That I again may kiss the lips
  Of him—my gallant one!

Dear Power of Love—that binds
Hearts to hearts, minds to minds,
In fond attachments all;
That cheers, though crimes appall—
Though earthquakes shake the soil,
And Mis'ry's wretches groan
'Midst Luxury and Toil;
That builds its rosy throne
On Nature's altitude alone!

Dear Power of Love! to thee
Succumbs Philosophy;
And men and angels are
Thy lamps, as sun and star
Are servant-orbs of God.
Within thy happy sway,
The presences that sod
And flow'ring wild display
Exalt the universal clay!

On a couch of texture
And caparison pure,
And elegant withal,
Zillora lay; a shawl
Her beauty's screen unvain.
Shy day-beams glittered through
The casement, and amain
Her closed eyes lit: swift flew
The shades,—the false before the true!

She woke, and the visions
Of her sleep derisions
Proved of existing life.
She was Vivanco's wife,
And mistress of his home—
No more a lonely sprite,
The shore and wood to roam,
And watch intently white
Sea-froths heave upward to the light.

Thus she called: " Constanza!"
Who, with kind undelay
Came: a maid whose calm sense
Zillora's confidence
Regaled; a servitor,
Yet worthily a friend.
Sympathy's greetings o'er,
Zillora to its end
Her story spoke—all hearts attend:

ZILLORA.

"Born on an ocean-isle,
My soul ne'er nurtured guile;
A queen I was, and free,
For man ne'er knelt to me;
From time-torn cliffs I gazed
O'er my beauteous domain:
The God of all I praised;
And when Affliction's pain
Aggrieved, I mourned, but laughed again!

"Oh, trance of mortal-morn,
When purest flowers adorn
The chalice of the soul!—
Methinks I see the roll
Of ocean, grand and high;
My father's cot, the rills
That murmur constantly;
The mountains and the hills—
My charms erst, whose charm instills!

"Blessing my maiden bloom,
Love sang through Nature's room
The tend'rest melody
That e'er enraptured me.
I little knew of man,
Save kindness paternal;
And never wished to scan
Brighter lands, more vernal,
Nor learnt that Life had phase infernal.

ZILLORA.

" One cloud-deserted day,
The deep impassive lay;
And out upon its breast
A ship appeared, at rest.
Anon, a boat the strand
Approached; a form unknown,
In raiment of command,
Stept on a wave-lashed stone,
And stood adventurous, alone.

" Elate, from bower of green,
I viewed the kindling scene,
And him who on the shore
Distinctive manhood wore;
And then exultant sped
To greet the household few;
And feeling-fluttered, said:
' Such sight I never knew—
A ship's anear, a stranger too!'

" A power unfelt before
My being claimed; 'twas more
Than hospitality;
'Twas tenderer than be
Passing courtesies, or
Fleet-changing emotion;
'Twas fostered in the core
Of my heart's devotion—
An islet fountain 'midst the ocean!

ZILLORA.

"We met,—the stranger-chief
And I—and Love's belief,
And mutual troth was ours.
In summer-vale of flowers
We vowed the happy pledge
To each the other bless:
Upon a lakelet's edge
We sat, and Life's distress
Was lost in Love's forgetfulness.

"No haunts by Vanity
Adorned can rival ye:
O elfin bowers of Love!
Expectancy did move
Me, when Vivanco told
Of other regions rare—
Far sunnier and less cold
Than that lone island, where
My innocence ne'er coped with care.

"My heart was not my own
Thenceforth a time; 'twas flown
To dear Vivanco's breast,
And soft by his caressed,
And given me anon
Metamorphosed, as 'twere,
By apt magician done!
Oh, Romance, debonair
And glowing, what a warmth was there!

"Away, away we came,
Within a twofold flame
Of Ecstasy and Hope.
Ah! then did I elope
From kindred ever fond—
Fonder as went the years—
To this abode, beyond
Their terror and their tears,
Their dreamy doubts and loving fears."

She finished; and her mien,
Saddened by Fancy's scene,
Wore Melancholy's token.
Beautiful, though broken,
Phœbus' flood was streaming
Through Zillora's boudoir;
And she, as from dreaming
Waked, up-gazed, and before
Her came a gentle visitor—

A rustic child, a girl,
With golden hair a-curl,
And tiny feet, and eyes,
That were for rhapsodies
Fit themes. To Zillora
She as a morning bliss
Was wont to come; and gay,
Yet sweetly unamiss,
She brought bloom-beauties and a kiss!

ZILLORA.

She brought full daintily,
Though not in filigree,
The fairest sisters of
The gardened vale and grove;
Intertwined with mosses
From the brook-shore, and shells,
Shaped like Christian crosses,
For chaste minds—wherein dwells
Affection for what Vice repels.

From basket of shore-reeds
Those treasures peeped—from weeds'
Embraces newly culled—
To smile, and then be dulled!
And Zillora placed them,
Dripping dews, in a vase,
Glossed with many a gem
And emblem of the race
From which Vivanco sprang, to grace.

The harmony of birds,
Attuned to cherubs' words,
Quavering down the air,
Spread gladness ev'rywhere;
And to Zillora gave
Fresh impetus of soul—
As winds the lolling wave
Bestir, till surges roll,
And flashing sprays enwreathe the whole!

Birds and flowers holy things
Oft memorize; the wings
Of Thought irradiant shine,
Upbearing themes divine,
Blest by their communion.
Oh, see! a vision now
Reveals a reunion—
Where rests the homely plow,
Where warblers chant and blossoms blow.

Humanity! in these
Creations, formed to please
The passion-fretted soul,
There is, though dirges toll
In slow, sad succession,
A happiness innate—
Nature's warm expression—
That bids bright Virtue wait
Erect, and Vice crouch to its fate.

Hark!—from the willow-dell
Chimes out the chapel bell,
Clear, solemn music, to
The many and the few.
How such sounds admonish
Mad revelers in guilt!—
But they none astonish,
In broad Christian lands, built
With altars, 'fore which fals'ties wilt.

ZILLORA.

Down an arched aisle of trees
And trellises, where bees
And orioles hummed and sung,
And floral drap'ries hung,
Zillora humbly sped—
Like an angel, earth-bound;
With her, faithful Hamed,
Her boy-companion, crowned
With favors, as with flowers the ground.

Her page he was, and mild,
Whom, when a tearful child,
Vivanco plucked from doom
Of ocean, and its gloom.
Wooing sublimity,
Nobleness he gained of
Manner and symmetry:
His thoughts for utt'rance strove
In melodies that sound above.

A bard forsooth! his lays
Zillora's saddened days
Diverted, and his sweet
Rhyme-numbers were discreet,
And flowed from Holiness—
True inspiration's fount.
Nature was his mistress—
Inspirer paramount!—
Whose charms he tired not to recount.

ZILLORA.

On smiles, by woman given,
Is reared the poet's heaven;
And though his passions rage
Infuriate, and wage
Their lustful war: o'er all,
E'en in the direst hour,
Beams a song-coronal,
Of intellectual dower,
That aye bespeaks the godlike power.

Th' empyrean o'er him,
The glories before him,
Around him, melting afar—
Where the linked mountains bar
The eye from the vast beyond,
And hem the Beautiful
In an azure-tint bond
Of dreams: from these to cull
Delight, he'd earth's base scenes annul!

Hastened to devotion
Zillora; commotion
Was in her breast, and calm
She would be; in the balm
Of worship sought she meek
Consolation.—But, lo!
Why quits her youthful cheek
Excitement's fervid glow?
Why shrinks she, as from 'venomed foe?

ZILLORA.

A form deformed, and clad
In monkish garb, that had
Wrapt worthier anchorite,
Aroused her full affright.
Though outwardly a monk,
A monk he was not; and
His soul, in passion sunk,
Was monstrous; for it planned
Deeds such as vilify a land.

When Innocence and Guilt
Are met, 'tis tilt and tilt,
If equal armed they are.
Perchance Guilt's scimitar
O'er Innocence's foil
Prevails awhile: oh, then,
Arise and dare turmoil,
Knight Honor—proud in men—
And maim and baffle Guilt again!

With gentleness, he strove
To lure the ear of Love;
And spoke thus gallantly:
"Sweet lady, I'd not thee
Detain; presumptuous 'twere
To wish the audience
Of humankind so fair;
Yet, ere thou goest hence,
Hear prophecy of consequence!"

Oh, prophecy as vile
As he whose soul of guile
Launched forth such grim decree!
'Twas told infernally.
Aghast Zillora stood,
As o'er Affection's urn;
For to her dearest blood
These deathly words did burn:
" Vivanco never will return!"

CANTO THIRD.

Noon, queen-hour of the light,
Put on her crown, and bright
Became the Eastern world.
Clouds lachrymose had whirled
Athwart the zenith, like
Mixed plumes, melting amain
From rays that gild and strike.
Noon—splendid be her reign—
Gloried the vales and hills of Spain.

And where tow'rd Italy
Spain looks across the sea,
Her gardens, groves, and vines
Resplendent spread: nor shines
More lustrous Nature's prime,
Of flower, and tree, and sky,
In lands of lesser crime—
Than shone afar and nigh
Castilia's fields and canopy.

ZILLORA.

Crows caw from pine and oak,
The oxen bear the yoke,
Elysium is unfound
Throughout terrestrial round;
But there is minted gold,
Earth's pageants to emboss:
So yellow, false, and cold—
Too oft the spirit's loss—
It gleams all human ways across.

Where hath Vivanco sped—
By Hope's swift phantoms led?
Where hath his fleet explored—
Intent on hidden hoard?
Love lit the chieftain's track:
Apart from all the rest,
Adieu he waved them back,
The sun upon his crest—
His ship's course veered to meet the West.

On, on, o'er Atlant's realm!—
Stanch the prow, true the helm,
Down the billows diving,
Up the billows striving,
Went the brave "Endeavor;"
And while vespers chanted
Praise of Life Forever,
'Mong far hills, saint-haunted,
Quick through twilight airs she panted!

ZILLORA.

Hail, hesperian Stars!
Venus is regnant, Mars
In Orient burns; and dies
The light along the skies—
The light sublimely beaming—
That lived from morn till eve.
Celestial atoms gleaming
During Phœbus' reprieve,
Ye twinkle hope to all that grieve!

The outcast lifts her face
From sin awhile, to trace
In your sodality
Her immortality.
Alas! that she should find
In but one hour of night
Themes fittest for the mind!
Alas! the mortal blight
That withers souls in Heaven's sight!

Upon a hill-side lone,
Whose less'ning shades were thrown
Like black robes on the lawn,
An old man sat at dawn—
A relic of the Day
That grappled Change, and died
Before the new away!—
A staff was at his side,
And down the wold his fleecy pride.

Calm as the scene, his eye—
Glancing anon on high,
And then earthward sinking—
Wandered; as though drinking
Soul-draughts from the fountains
Of ethereal Hope,
Fortitude from mountains,
Patience from plain and slope;
And through the vales his mind would grope

In thoughts of many themes,
That deepened into dreams
And phantasms of the tomb:
Till, 'midst the lily-bloom
And rose emblazonry,
That bowered plain and wood,
Where streamlets poured to sea,
Roused Recollection stood,—
A sorrowed angel, there to brood!

A shout upon the coast;
A trumpet sound that's lost
In echoes 'mong the hills;
A ship, whose broad sail fills
With inward breezes soft,
To her moorings speeding:
Casting the spray aloft—
Waves aplay impeding—
Oh, 'twas dignity exceeding!

ZILLORA.

All these the watcher heard
And saw, nor uttered word;
But grasped his staff, and rose
Benignant in his woes.
Adown the copse-screened glen,
And o'er the clovered green,
He journeyed: then, oh, then,
His visage, pale of sheen,
Revealed delight—long, long unseen.

Oh, mightily rejoice—
United heart and voice
Of city, hamlet, home—
When tidings gladsome come
Of famous wanderer!
Those of the wayward child
Inspire a holier
Joy; that beams like the mild
Young day, through nightly storm-clouds wild!

And such Vivanco told
Of sweet Zillora; bold
He was forsooth before
Her kindred—on the floor
Where danced her girlhood-feet.
Brave and proud, yet tender,
He walked the village-street,
Zillora's defender—
Till e'en gossips would commend her!

ZILLORA.

And the maidens they laughed,
While the peasant swains quaffed
Their draughts of jovial wine.
The sea's ecstatic brine,
In phosphorescent waves,
Vied with the landscape's smile.
There oped anear no graves
That morn, and the dread wile
Of Death seemed banished from the isle.

What whim of yearning age
Impelled the hill-side sage—
Zillora's antique sire?—
His spirit flamed with fire
Of resurrected dreams,
That verified old Love
Undying. Ah! there beams
Unchanged, below, above,
But Nature's truth her truth to prove.

He prayed beside a mound,
Hedged and violet-crowned:
A wreath of rosemary
Was held in his chary
Embrace—Zillora's gift.
His eyes were tear-bedimmed,
As under the blue lift
He knelt, and his locks rimmed
The sod, by bounteous beauty limned.

ZILLORA.

A tear, a smile, a kiss:
Brief change from grief to bliss,
From bliss to grief; and yet
'Tis hopeless to forget
Grief in joy, joy in grief.
There died not king or slave,
There lives not serf or chief,
That felt not, feels not grave
And glad emotions raise, deprave!

It was the rest of one—
Than whom this world has none
More pure in loving, true
In trials, blisses too!—
Like whom there's no other
On earth, in Heaven, so dear—
A kind, pious mother.
And that spot revered sear
And green had grown many a year.

Zillora's mother there
Slept beneath that mound, fair
With cultured grass and flowers.
How oft the duty's ours,
Oh, fellow-men, in deep,
Yet conscious reverie,
To wander and to weep,
'Midst hills and by the sea,
O'er ashes of mortality!

ZILLORA.

Speak! eyes that flash and burn—
Speak! eyes that melt and mourn:
What are ye, if not stars
Diverse—suggesting wars,
And stimulating Peace?
Forever as the years
Successively increase,
Will human eyes glance fears,
Hopes, hates, and melt in love and tears!

Vivanco's mission o'er,
He left the island shore,
And sailed away—away
Eastward, bosoming a
Primrose cross, pansy-dyed;
And when the darkness palled,
He looked over the wide
Ocean, firmament-walled,
And listened as a night-voice called:

"Love's triumph is thine own:
Arise! face Virtue's throne;
Renounce thy lust of gold;
In Charity behold
Thy labors, broadly blest.
Zillora will be nigh:
The cross upon her breast;
Her smiles will glorify
Thy worth throughout Futurity!"

ZILLORA.

In search of treasure-trove,
What perils, rudely wove,
Beset the buccaneer.—
Warily doth he steer
Tow'rd land : when out at sea,
How boldly wings his ship,
From hull to topmast free!
Ah! outlaw, thou shalt sip
Of av'rice, though it burn thy lip!

Revert thee, mindful strain,
To noonday o'er old Spain;
To noonday 'mong the hills,
Musical with the trills
Of woodland choristry :
Where, ancient as the Moors,
An abbey, ruined, wry
And moldering, allures
Most picturesquely, and assures

The skeptic: As decay
Blurs Nature's grandest day
So in the soul's full glow
Live memories of woe,
And shrinking dread of Death.
Since all that's human errs,
Preserving Virtue's breath,
No miracle occurs
When skeptics turn philosophers

Among the abbey-tombs,
Indicative of dooms,
Sat fierce Dendari,
Vivanco's deputy.
In meditation grim
He pondered; and the shades
Of death-marks threatened him!
And records, some of maids,
Moralized from the rent arcades.

Why paused he there in the
Golden light, musingly?
He waited bounty rich,
Filched from treasure-trove, which,
Vaulted deep, his day-dream
Was, and nightly vision.
He lingered, and the stream
Of mem'ry whelmed decision—
Stygian 'twas, not, not elysian!

Ay! treasure-trove was sought
By slaves half-score, and taught
Of Mammon, 'mong the dead.
The flowers beneath their tread
Were crushed upon the turf;
And still Dendari lurked
Apart, waiting the surf
Of Fortune: though it irked
His temper, wherein tumults worked.

ZILLOBA.

They found gilt treasure-trove—
They found the miser's love,
The spendthrift's plaything—gold:
Of quaint, religious mold.
And dark Dendari smiled;
But the heavens frowned,
And clouds in legions wild
Shut sunshine from the ground—
Where Desecration's sight and sound

Held sacrilegious feast.
The tempest-signs increased;
And as the buccaneers,
Down borne by pelf and fears,
Swept from the land their prize,
Loud thunders noised aloft,
Sharp lightnings cleft the skies,
And airs, erst perfumed, soft,
Waxed vengeful, and their sweetness doffed.

The elements that blew
Dendari and his crew,
Conspired to crush and blast
Those lives; and shook each mast
Of the doomed ship, and hurled
Abroad, with angry sweep,
A wreck to warn the world!
All, all, a woeful heap,
Sank to the valleys of the deep!

ZILLORA.

1.

Oh, guardian spirits of the Good—
    Alert in light of holy ray—
Watch o'er his hours of solitude;
    And when temptations crowd the way,
Breathe on his soul, and keep him true
    To country, friends, and native loam—
His heart to blest endeavors woo,
    And urge the wanderer home.

2.

A trusty welcome waits him there:
    Though 'tis alone a wife's embrace
That wreathes with Love his breast of care,
    How dear becomes the lowliest place!
Winds, waves, and sails propitious be—
    While sunshine sparkles on the foam,
That crests the billows of the sea—
    And bear the wanderer home!

On, on, o'er the shining
Waters, truth-divining,
Dashed dauntless Vivanco—
Whilom the proud bravo,
And eager merchantman.
These no more; for his soul
All attributes would ban,
That covet worldly dole;
And thus unerring seek its goal.

Uprose the headland heights
Of home,—aye gladsome sights!
And from the harbor clear,
Stretched meadow, brake, and mere,
To the peace-throned mountains.
Within the castle, from
Shore-land groves and fountains,
On earth, in air, the hum
Of Joy announced the chief had come.

Grief shrunk, a demon-thing,
When Joy, re-wakening,
Immersed in shadeless beams
Zillora's life; whose dreams
Of bliss had come only
Faint glimmering through woe—
Singly, ghostly, lonely.—
She cried, her form aglow:
"'Tis he, 'tis my lord Vivanco!"

He heard, he saw, he knew
Her greeting, joyful, true;
He looked into her eyes,
Illumed by ecstasies,
And viewed Heaven's radiance there;
He clasped her to his heart,
And smoothed her waving hair.
Though Destiny should thwart
Resolve, they ne'er again would part!

Designing gentle deeds,
They searched the peasants' needs
Together; ev'ry morn
New charities were born,
And the chapel-bell
Rang pæans of happy-day !
Hamed sublimely sang :
Zillora, meekly gay,
Vivanco cherished, loved alway.

GATHERINGS OF SONG.

I.

THE HUDSON RIVER.

I.

O, RIVER of resplendent life,
    Thee buoyantly I sing;
And to thy native glories rife
    Fond recognition bring.

II.

'Mong rocks and bowers, past grove and grange,
    The Hudson rolls in pride;
Majestic is the bloomy range
    That binds its mighty tide.

III.

Behold its bosom, sail-bedecked;
  Its borders, woodland-crowned;—
How placidly its depths reflect
  The arching sky and ground!

IV.

Walls, chiseled by fair Nature's hand,
  Defy the shocks of Time;
They rise above the brilliant strand,
  As barricades sublime.

V.

The Palisades' unbending tower;
  The Highlands, gray or green,
Complacent stand, as things of power—
  The nestling vales between.

VI.

The vision drinks the landscaped view,
  With ecstasy enthralled;
The mountain-tops melt 'mid the blue,
  By wide horizon walled.

VII.

No dark and tott'ring ruins grace
  Each promontory's brow;
Dear Beauty beams in Nature's face,
  Unrivaled in its glow!

VIII.

Rich domes surmount the monarch hills,
    The cottage lies below;
From far-off fountains many rills
    Down to the river flow.

IX.

Upon its wild, romantic banks,
    Art swiftly hews its way;
And boldly thins the forest ranks,
    Where songsters greet the day.

X.

The produce of the fertile West
    Finds passage to the coast;
The ocean billows smoothly rest
    And in its calm are lost.

XI.

The woodman's song full joyous swells
    Along the peaceful shore;
Neat villages usurp the dells,
    The heights are peopled o'er!

XII.

The cattle stray along the brink,
    That Hudson's waters lave;
They stoop in quietude, and drink
    From brooks that swell its wave.

XIII.

The red man nevermore shall hold
   This river of his sires;
No, no, his birthright now is sold,
   And quenched the council-fires!

XIV.

Brave Science walks the varied land,
   And hopeful Honor strives;
Civilization lifts its wand,
   Yet Nature's charm survives!

XV.

Sweet Flora plants her children on
   The slopes that meet the wave;
The flow'rets blush, and fade anon
   Into the earth that gave.

XVI.

Amid those scenes by Romance lit,
   The ardent brain is fired:
The painter's touch grows exquisite,
   The poet wakes inspired.

XVII.

When Night shades mountains, dales, and meres,
   And flames her lanterns far,
In bord'ring homes each lamp-light cheers—
   The rival of each star!

XVIII.

Oh, oft have lovers vowed their love
   Beside this cherished stream;
And o'er its banks together rove,
   When youth seems as a dream.

XIX.

Live, live, ye bursting woodland springs,
   That Hudson's tide supply;
Fly, fly, ye crafts, on breeze-swept wings,
   Smile bright above, O sky!

XX.

Thou River, grand and mountain-born,
   That Genius loves to scan,
Roll on, till angel-trumpets warn,
   A proud delight to man!

MOONLIGHT ON THE HUDSON.

I.

There's moonlight on the river-wave,
  It glitters down the tide;
Our hearts are gladsome, young, and brave,
  And merrily we glide.
The shimm'ring beams illume the shore,
And brightly touch each dripping oar—
A soul-blent melody we pour
     Over the waters wide.

II.

The ripples, tinged with mildest light,
  Enchant us as we row;
And maiden eyes, bewitching, bright,
  Seem dearer in their glow.
Sweet music comes, of heavenly tone,
Across the Hudson, calm and lone,
And echoes from the hills are thrown,
     And fainter, fainter grow.

III.

Black shadows slumber 'mid the vales,
   And rest within the grove;
Behind the Highlands play the gales,
   Serenity's above.
Row gently, brothers! may yon beam,
That flashes on the glorious stream,
Wake in our hearts a conscious gleam
   Of purity and love.

IV.

Oh! joyously we onward float
   O'er Hudson's depths of blue;
And kindly urge our little boat
   With loving hearts and true.
High in the heavens dear Luna shines,
More lustrous far than gem-strewn mines;
At morn she all her light resigns—
   Ah, then, adieu, adieu!

NATIVE HILLS.

I.

Native Hills, how I love ye,
   High over the river;
With your green crowns above ye,
   As brilliant as ever.
'Mong your woodlands and waters
   Sweet beauties recline;
And the smiles of your daughters
   Seem always divine.

II.

On your brows of fresh glory
   I gaze long admiring;
For ye tell me the story
   My heart was desiring:
A mute story of sweetness,
   Of love and true joy,
And of bright years of fleetness,
   When I was a boy.

III.

Cold Boreas may sear ye,
  Yet summer will gladden;
Oh, 'tis bliss to be near ye,
  Though all the world sadden!
For an innocence blesses
  Your flower-scented wild,
In the zephyr-caresses
  Of breezes unguiled!

IV.

Native Hills, how I love ye,
  So noble and blooming;
With your green crowns above ye,
  Wide grandeur assuming.
Full of love is my greeting:
  From my heart lifts the pall—
As of yore, it is beating,
  Proud Hills, for ye all!

THE WOODLAND BRIDGE.

I.

APART from the village, in the woodland,
　Spanning a wide ravine,
Above the brook's volume, rurally planned,
　An olden bridge is seen.
There oftentimes I rest,
When sunshine fills the West,
　To list to songs attuned 'mid haunts of green.

II.

From brink to brink, it arches o'er the glen,
　Of rustic form, more dear;
The squirrel skips in timid awe of men,
　And quick, instinctive fear
There lovers sweetly meet,
To earnest love repeat,
　While Peace reigns mistress of the woody sphere.

III.

The forest trees in multitudes arise,
   And at their feet smile flowers;
Paths wind among, unseen by summer-skies,
   From the bridge to the bowers;
The brook-tide murmurs songs,
Each bedded rock prolongs
    The cadence soft, thrilling the peaceful hours.

IV.

Fair rears the woodland round that lone bridge rude—
   Blest spot where joys agree!
There's loveliness amid the solitude
   Of grassy vale and tree;
There shines a tender sheen
Above that deep ravine,
    That lifts the soul to sentiment and glee.

BUDS AND BLOSSOMS.

I.

Buds and blossoms, buds and blossoms—
   First bright off'rings of the year—
Bathed in raindrops, all your bosoms
   Burst within the sunlight clear.
Joyously my heart-voice greets ye—
   Buds and blossoms, as I gaze
On your unenduring beauty,
   Harbingers of sunny days!

II.

Nature's sweet and ripening treasure
   Shyly to the world appears;
Soon 'twill be of fullest measure,
   Laughingly, oft dripping tears!
Beauteous tints in blushing glory
   Grace the woodland and the mead:
Golden, green, and colors gory
   Kindest admiration plead.

III.

Strong-limbed trees, and bush, and bramble,
    Spring-tide's gorgeous mantles wear;—
How I love betimes to ramble
    'Mid the blooming wild-wood fair!
Brooklets sparkle still more brightly
    As they dash o'er moss and stone;
Human hearts beat cheerful, lightly,
    Earth seems glad, harsh winds have flown.

IV.

Fleet-winged birds, on branches singing,
    Tune their voices sweetest now;
For the buds green leaves are bringing,
    And the blossoms fruitful grow.
See the valleys and the meadows,
    Dipped in fragrance all their own,
Granting sunlight-circled shadows
    To this season-changing zone!

V.

Friendly showers, the heavens resigning,
    Buds and blossoms freshly lave—
Softly pure, of blest designing,
    Smiling o'er their annual grave.
Smiling round the gaudy palace,
    Smiling round the cottage fair—
On the cliffs, and up the trellis,
    Buds and blossoms everywhere!

VI.

Just above the grass-tops growing,
   Peep the tender infant flowers;
Ev'ry little leaflet glowing
   In its peaceful pristine bowers.
Within the heart, Hope, full cheery,
   Radiates the spirit-gloom:
Earthly scenes are never dreary
   In the rapture of their bloom!

A WAIF.

Broad-cultured grounds, artistic, grand,
  Where lingers rich, exotic grace,
Inspire not, as divinely planned;
  No, no, 'tis in the forest-space—
Where, unconfined, dear Nature smiles-
  That scenes appear, by Mem'ry kept:
Firm as the beauteous tropic isles,
  By billows of the ocean swept!

SUMMER.

I.

FAIR Summer speeds over the earth
  In the chariot of Time,
And fosters the 'wakening worth
  Of all its verdure sublime.
    The meadows grow greener,
    The heavens serener,
  And purer the changing clime.

II.

Its paths, with the Beautiful strewn,
  Spread far from highland to sea,
And taste the soft brightness of June,
  And thrill with its melody;
    Alluring the lover
    And gentle maid over,
  To where sips the gauze-winged bee!

III.

The flow'rets their eyelids unclose,
  And gaze askance and around;
The lily peeps shyly; the rose
  Seems proud, though blushing profound;
    And the fleet warblers fly
    On the breath of July,
  And brooks sing low to the ground.

IV.

The heart is delighted, nor feels,
  As glowing August revives,
The impulse of sorrow, till steals
  Fair Summer away, and gyves
    Of the Frost-king surround.
    Ah! then earth seems a mound—
  A chill comes over our lives!

VIOLETS AND PANSIES.

I.

Far above the glowing river,
   Where dear Nature plies her loom,
Smiling upward to the Giver,
   Violets and pansies bloom;
Soon beneath the snow to shiver,
   Beauteous ere their chilly doom!

II.

Bright are violets and pansies,
   Of cerulean-crimson hues;
Luring fond and tender fancies,
   As ascending perfume wooes!
Clustered as the dawn advances,
   Gleaming in the crystal dews.

III.

Beautiful, yet modest-seeming,
    Beam they 'mong their sister flowers,
While the lake anear is gleaming,
    Mirroring its banks and bowers,
And the morning light is streaming
    Down upon the lawns and towers.

IV.

Plucked by hands unseared by toiling,
    Sunny tresses they adorn;
And on breasts of Love, love-foiling,
    Lie they, from Earth's bosom torn;
Fading, dying, crisping, spoiling,
    Cast away to Death forlorn!

V.

Violets and pansies ever,
    Drinking deep of Phœbus grand,
Swell the sweetness of that river,
    And its bloom-enveloped strand,
Smiling upward to the Giver,
    Nurtured by His heavenly hand!

MORNING-GLORIES.

I.

Decking, with their sister-blooms,
    Garden, grove, and lawn;
Flushing Nature's verdant rooms,
    Lit by early dawn,
Morning-glories strew the land,
Clinging upward, zephyr-fanned.

II.

Pretty, in profusion wild,
    Twining 'midst the trees,
Peeping out where rocks compiled
    Sentinel the leas,
Morning-glories taste the clime,
Searing with the Summer-time.

III.

Children wreathe them into crowns,
　Crimson, purple, blue;
Maidens cull them for their gowns,
　Thoughtless what they do;
For ere the nightly damps descend,
Decay despoils, and breezes rend!

IV.

Pleasures rule the dance and feast,
　Pleasures flash round wine;
But oh! methinks they are increased
　Where morning-glories shine.
There Peace and Health their sweets unfold,
Around the hills, adown the wold!

SONG OF THE MOWERS.

I.

Let us go unto the mowing,
For the eastern sky is glowing
    With the morn;
Dull drowsiness shall not be ours,
While fields and dales are bright with flowers,
    Grass and corn;
No, no, grasp firm the scythe and sickle—
Though toil-drops down our foreheads trickle,
  To labor we were born.

II.

Our garments are uncouth and coarse,
But then our breasts know not remorse
    For wrong deeds.
We swing our many steels full keen,
And sever all the blades of green
    On the meads;
And grasping firm the scythe and sickle,
We feel, as toil-drops brightly trickle,
  We labor for our needs.

III.

The Summer is our time of joy,
When Nature's scenes young hearts decoy—
    Wide and grand.
Oh, let us cheer our work with song,
And while the echoes sound along
    Down the land,
Let's firmly grasp the scythe and sickle,
And feel, as toil-drops warmly trickle,
    New vigor in each hand.

IV.

Our modest homes are ever blent
With gentleness and true content,
    'Mid life's blast.
List, list unto the cheerful call
Of voices by the garden wall—
    To repast.
Let fall the flashing scythe and sickle,
Dash off the toil-drops as they trickle—
    We've mown the field at last!

AUTUMN.

I.

'Tis Autumn, and the fresh green leaves
    Grow yellow, pale and sear;
The grain is housed—packed up in sheaves—
    For wint'ry days are near.

II.

The blooming Summer-time has fled,
    And growing plants mature;
Jack Frost will soon uprear his head
    To torture rich and poor!

III.

The fruits in tempting clusters cling,
    And lusciously they fall,
As rough'ning winds the brown leaves fling
    On meadow, stream, and mall.

IV.

The flowers in dying beauty hang
    Where erst they flourished sweet;
The birds, that on the tree-tops sang,
    Fly South on pinions fleet.

V.

The farmer gathers in his store
    That Industry supplies,
And fondly looks the furrows o'er
    Where grew his summer-prize.

VI.

The varied hues of Autumn-time,
    How fair, yet sad are they—
Embellishing the world sublime,
    And warning of decay!

VII.

O, kindly season of the year,
    Though sadness robes you round,
Abundance gives the warmth and cheer
    That in your heart is found!

OCTOBER.

I.

October, hail! I see thy sign,
   So heraldic of Nature's woe,
In things that darkle, things that shine,
   Anear, afar, above, below.

II.

The forest seems a mighty flame,
   Whose leafy sparks gleam down the air,
And huddle in their dying shame,
   'Midst hills and vales, and here and there.

III.

And o'er the heart an influence steals,
   Not gay, nor yet of bitter grief,
But such methinks the oak-tree feels,
   When parting with its first dead leaf!

IV.

Sonorous, on the matin-breeze,
    Come sounds from o'er the river-waves;
Now loud, then less'ning by degrees,
    Like lives, that end in distant graves.

V.

O, thoughtful time! October, thee
    I deem the mentor of the year;
For thou its grandest change doth see,
    And smil'st its smile, and shed'st its tear.

VI.

And mem'ries that reposed in Spring,
    And slept throughout the Summer's glow,
Awake, and ope their wings, and fling
    Their pliant shadows 'cross my brow.

VII.

Then come, October, when thou wilt,
    Magnificent beneath the sun;
The heavens are with thy glory gilt,
    Dies on Earth's breast her beauteous one!

THE FALL OF THE LEAVES.

I.

How mournful and meek is the fall of the leaves,
As prayerful Autumn with fortitude grieves
For Summer, her sister, immured in the grave:
    The winds shriek over her,
    The dun leaves cover her,
And bleak is the landscape, and dark is the wave.

II.

There's a monody in the fall of the leaves,
As downward they flit to their cousins the sheaves,
Broadcast and withering on hill-side and plain;
    As heaped in the valley,
    Whose trees creak dismally,
Bereft of their beauty, lamenting disdain.

III.

No harmonies joy o'er the fall of the leaves,
And the sorry-eyed sprite of the woodland weaves
A chaplet of decay for the Autumn-king.
    'Tis Love now gladdens all,
    For Nature saddens all,
And I turn from the scene to dream of the Spring.

GATHERINGS OF SONG.

WINTER'S VICTIM.

I.

Ah, crony mine, alone we sit,
   While round us howls the Winter,
And thoughts of Beauty dying flit,
   As sparks from yonder splinter.
Earth, air, and sky are bleak and chill—
   Blest Virgin guide the comer,
Who ventures o'er this Highland hill—
   The monument of Summer.

II.

Relight your meerschaum, crony mine,
   Let's dream in clouds together;
Refill your glass with friendly wine,
   We'll toast the summer-weather.
For oh, wild frosts shall ne'er congeal,
   Nor make our hearts the glummer,
Nor blight the kindness that we feel
   For earth-delighting Summer.

III.

Hark! heard you not a cry full faint,
    Yet loud to ears of pity?
Ope, ope the door, no human plaint
    Shall pass us to the city.
What's here? a girl and aged man—
    He guards but to benumb her—
'Tis Winter, shivering and wan,
    And 'neath his robes the Summer.

IV.

Come in, come in, thou hoary form,
    Come in, thou frozen beauty;
Here glows the firelight glad and warm,
    With hearts of tender duty.
Take thou the farthest ingle-rest,
    Weird sage, where thou may'st slumber;
The girl I'll cherish to my breast,
    In burning love of Summer!

V.

And crony mine—the embers fade,
    A frost is in my bosom—
Alas! she's dead, my lovely maid:
    White-haired! but why accuse him?
He sleeps as with a soul of grace,
    With mien than erst not grummer—
Haste, haste thee, comrade, seek a place,
    Where we may bury Summer.

VI.

Lost Bloom! the North-wind moans her dirge,
  Be ours to aye commend her;
But grieve not, comrade, she'll emerge
  From out the grave in splendor.
She'll rise again, and charm the world;
  Then, wand'ring never from her,
We'll laugh to see old Winter hurled
  From all the paths of Summer!

II.

SWEET IS THE SONG.

I.

Sweet is the song that Love inspires;
  There are no sweeter strains on earth
Than those that flow from dear desires,
  And charm attachments into birth.
They pleasure Grief and soften Mirth,
  And, trilling from unnumbered lyres,
Resound in hearts beside the hearth,
  Rebound to souls of fiercer fires!

II.

Sweet is the song that Friendship fills
  With kindliness that ne'er reproves—
Amid a wilderness of ills
  Spread blooming gardens, pleasant groves,
In smiles and words that hallow loves.
  Souls cling to souls, as vales to hills,
And night or noonday ne'er removes
  The union of harmonious wills.

BEAUTY.

A VISION of light rose before me—
   'Twas Beauty's, forever divine;
Enchanting illusions came o'er me,
   To Beauty more brightly define.
The mold and the grace of each feature
   Woke ev'ry fond feeling of mine:
"Oh, dwells there on earth such a creature—
   Bends she at Humanity's shrine?"
Dear Beauty told not of her mission,
   But smiles lit her visage benign;
She vanished, as flitted the vision,
   And left me in darkness to pine.
Come again, sweet vision of bliss from above,
   Flee not so hastily, charmer of Love!

FRIENDSHIP.

I.

When Friendship glitters in each eye,
   And warms the pressure of each hand,
Misfortune's weights more lightly lie,
   And crumbling, yield like desert sand.
They fall from off the tortured heart—
   Ill-judged, despised, condemned o'ermuch—
And, as dark memories, depart
   At Friendship's true and gen'rous touch.

II.

Oh! 'tis an hour of misery—
   Yet many souls that hour withstand—
When Friendship's gleam grows shadowy,
   And dead its pulse in ev'ry hand.
At such a time, be calm, sad heart,
   Be prayerful, be very meek;
Thy faith will shield from mortal dart,
   And glad the soul, and flush the cheek!

MEETING AND PARTING.

I.
'Twas a mild fair night in the bud of the year,
And the lamps of the village were burning near.

II.
The stream was silvered, for unveiled was the moon,
And the birds of the woodland had hushed their tune.

III.
Hills, meadows, and mountains were dim, though the Night
Was ne'er before blest with more sparkles of light.

IV.
There stept o'er the pathway a maidenly form,
Her spirit aglow, and love-bursting and warm.

V.
'Twas Lelia, and half-affrighted she peered
Through the dew-blent air, as if something she feared.

VI.
To a vine-trellised arbor noiseless she sped,
She neared it—'twas still as a place of the dead.

VII.

The dead was afar, but the living was there—
Young Ormond, her lover, with dark wavy hair.

VIII.

He awaited Lelia, thoughtful and lone,
As the moon's soft beams on his countenance shone.

IX.

Bright blossoms illumined the boughs that o'erhung,
But thoughtless he was of the beauties among.

X.

Thoughts came with a burning he could not control,
Of Lelia, the light and joy of his soul.

XI.

A footfall, advancing, came over the lawn,
As timid and quick as the tread of a fawn.

XII.

Two hearts throbbed tenderly within the still shade—
In Love they were one, and in Honor unfrayed.

XIII.

They met but to part in that trim trysting-place,
And glad was their greeting, and dear their embrace.

XIV.

Two roses were linked in the turf at their feet—
A symbol of hearts when their love is complete.

XV.

"Though goest thou, Ormond, where Peace is defiled,
I'll await thee, as now, as pure and unguiled."

XVI.

Thus Lelia sighed, and her Ormond as true,
Plucked from the green sod the linked roses that grew.

XVII.

" I give thee this flow'ret, and this I retain,
'Twill 'mind thee, Lelia, of me on the main."

XVIII.

Love's tear-drops commingled their kiss of adieu :
They parted, and vanished from mutual view.

XIX.

The moon sank down into the vastness of Night,
And the lamps of the village revealed no light.

XX.

Lelia is sad, and full often she weeps,
But the love of Ormond she faithfully keeps !

GATHERINGS OF SONG.

LA SEÑORITA.

A ROMANCE.

I.

Journeying near that cherished river,
The rushing, gushing Guadalquivir,
   Where Summer meets reviving Spring,
   I heard La Señorita sing;
And oh! whenever griefs are mine,
That Spanish mem'ry warms like wine,
   And gives to Thought a sunny wing!

II.

Among the orange-boughs I listened,
While the stream below purely glistened,
   And laved the glowing esplanade;
   Then I peered through the perfumed shade,
And bright-eyed Señorita saw:
Her beauty forced a tender awe,
   In simple sanctity displayed.

GATHERINGS OF SONG.

III.

As beamed each scene of ancient story,
She sang of Moorish love and glory,
   But knew not that, o'erheard by me,
   She swelled another's ecstasy.
Sweet from an amaranthine bower
Her utt'rance charmed me, as a flower,
   Whose exhalations lure the bee!

IV.

My heart awoke to soft emotion—
'Twas Passion mingled with Devotion—
   An impulse of a fond unrest,
   That, momentary, made me blest.
Ah! he that such grace could not woo,
No tingling of Love ever knew,
   Nor felt a quick throb in his breast!

V.

Alas! a scrutinizing señor,
Of flashing glance, and proud demeanor,
   La Señorita led away.
   I watched them down the garden stray,
And o'er my being fell a gloom—
'Twill haunt my spirit to the tomb,
   Until my body joins the clay!

ON THE LAKE.

I.

Swift o'er the lake the light boat moves,
    With Youth and Beauty freighted,
Past shrubby headlands, floral coves,
    So picturesquely mated—
Past rustic houses on the shore,
    And lovers roving, resting,
And children gath'ring more and more,
    The slopes and arches cresting.

II.

The sky is of a cloudless blue—
    The waters ripple brightly;
The boatman dips his paddles true—
    They sparkling rise, and lightly;
And now in sunshine, now in shade,
    While gliding hither, thither,
Sweet Youth and Beauty, heaven-made,
    A heaven make together!

III.

Anon they step upon the land,
    A land of summer-glory;
No blight before, on either hand,
    No scenes decayed or hoary;
But all is green, and grand, and bright,
    And Youth and Beauty roaming
Down od'rous dale, up healthful height,
    Rejoice until the gloaming.

AFFECTION FOR NATURE.

I.

The fervor of Love may be maddened,
The heart of the lover be saddened,
   By the scorn of her he adored;
Earth's round may seem black to him,
Till her love comes back to him,
   And clings to the soul it ignored;
But there's an affection that maddens not,
So calm in the heart that it saddens not,
It quickens at home, and 'tis cherished abroad,
For landscapes and waters where Nature is lord.

II.

The dew-drops that moisten the morning,
The ocean, whose thunderlike warning
   Comes crashing from billowy brine—
Creations that charmingly
'Midst woodlands and mountains be,
   Are glorious lovers of mine!
Their converse exalts, and thoughts upheaving
Pluck inspiration from sweets inweaving,
And their mingled presences shadow and shine
With beauty and majesty almost divine.

A SKETCH.

I.

She moved 'mong friends dear and beloved,
   Within her vine-encircled home;
Her smile a double welcome proved
   To all that to her home had come.
True joyousness controlled each heart,
   Kind greetings 'work a gentler thrill;
And Friendship, pure and free from art,
   To ev'ry bosom brought good-will.

*   *   *   *   *   *

II.

Alas! dark Sorrow wraps the scene—
   That matron, friend and darling one
   Lies cold in death—the morrow's sun
Shines on her grave, o'ertopped with green.
And those that but a day agone
   Felt impulse of a lively mirth,
Habiliments of mourning don,
   And weep for her, released from earth!

THE PURE AND THE LOVELY.

I.

Oh, grant me the Pure and the Lovely,
  Angelical One;
Oh, grant me the Pure and the Lovely,
  That my heart, sorrow-rifted,
  May be joyously lifted
    To the smile of the Saviour Son—
That Beauty, in robes of the Holy,
May beam o'er my spirit, full lowly,
    Till its moments of earth are done.

II.

Oh, grant me the Pure and the Lovely,
  Angelical One;
Oh, grant me the Pure and the Lovely,
  When the rays of Aurora
  Cheer the children of Flora,
    And shadows all the hill-tops shun—
When the fiery orb at even
Retires adown the western heaven,
    Beneath clouds celestially spun.

III.

Oh, grant me the Pure and the Lovely,
 Angelical One;
Oh, grant me the Pure and the Lovely;
 For the blooms of the highland,
 And the maid of the island,
  I'd claim, as the day the sun!
Oh, grant to my heart living Gladness,
Till outcast and fugitive Sadness
  Shall shrink like a specter undone!

MY BEAUTIFUL ANGEL.

I.

She was my beautiful angel,
　The soul of my hopes and my dreams;
A bright and beautiful angel,
　She high in Eternity beams.
She gained the Blest Land before me,
　Away from all passion and guile;
Methinks she yet watches o'er me,
　Like a star o'er a lonely isle.

II.

She flew away in the morning,
　And my heart with sorrow was gloomed;
Her mem'ry shines a sweet warning
　O'er many earth-blisses entombed,
O'er hopes all hopeless forever,
　O'er dreams that were lost when she died;
Oh! my life's a cheerless river,
　And brambles envelop its side!

III.

The flowers that smile in the valleys
   Are ever the saddest when near;
They'mind me of gentle Alice,
   Who died in the chill of the year:
For as the last rose to ashes
   Dropt dull on the withering sod,
She closed her light-sealing lashes,
   And her soul soared upward to God!

MARY.

I.

Sister of my budding life,
    Sister of my manhood's bloom,
Sister when dear joys are rife,
    Sister when o'erblackens Gloom!
Still thou art my sister sweet,
    Still my heart's enduring light,
Still the list'ner for my feet,
    In the chill, tempestuous night—
                Mary!

II.

Thou, most noble spirit-friend,
    Thou, companion of the Past,
Thou, whose words of patience lend
    Heart-hope, when Despair would blast—
Thou'rt my star of cheerfulness,
    As in thought I nightly stroll;
And methinks, when joys caress,
    I'm a fragment of thy soul—
                Mary!

III.

WAR.

I.

Pulsing in violent, feverish throbs,
  Wildly, recklessly dashing,
Life flows red, and its groans and its sobs
  Follow the saber's clashing.
The tufts of the plain,
  The rocks of the height,
Bear up the brave slain,
  As battle's fierce light
    'Midst pallid smoke is flashing.

II.

Horsemen and infantry rush to the shock,
  Storming, defending, flying,
And shouts of "Victory" cruelly mock
  The pangs of soldiers dying.
The thunders of strife,
  On morning's sweet breath,
Now quicken warm Life,
  Now horrify Death,
    While hearts afar are sighing.

III.

As bivouac-fires, through lengthening years
   Illume grand woodlands nightly,
I pray that joy may follow the tears,
   That trickle sad, yet brightly—
That flowers may upbreathe
   O'er warrior-graves;
And war-ships, beneath
   Oceanic waves,
     Decay unseen, unsightly!

BATTLE OF LOOKOUT MOUNTAIN.

October 28, 1863.

I.

Defiantly on Lookout Mount the Rebel soldiers spread,
And in the valley confident the Fed'ral legions tread;
Brave Hooker guides their fearless march, true Howard's in the van,
And Geary guards the valley-road, as only hero can.
As steadfast as the ocean-rock that curbs the tempest-sea,
His troops resist the battle-wave, and keep the mastery.
In giant grandeur stand the heights from which rebuffs are hurled,
And Longstreet flaunts an upstart flag that desecrates the world!
The morning beam is tinging faint the merry mountain rills,
Resounding volleys crash aloft, and echo 'mong the hills,
Proud Lookout looms discordant, dim,—a flaming pile of war,—
Its woods the hideous haunts of Death, its sod a couch of gore.

II.

From glen and cliff and shelt'ry trench the hostile thunders peal;
They rouse the heart, they mad the brain to potency of zeal;
They quicken ev'ry sense of rage that slumbers in the soul,
As Carnage flames its ghastly torch, and lurid flames uproll!
How fiercely meet those kindred forms, how dreadful, yet sublime
The scene whereon red Murder stalks to expiate a crime!
Ah! thus it is, man bleeds to purge the follies of his kind,
And writhing, dies in butchered plight, his groan upon the wind.
Hark! from the Mountain's crimsoned side reverberates the strife,
And Smith's Brigade ascends the steep to offer life for life.
They bear the Union's banner high—it glitters as a charm—
There's patriotism in each heart, and valor in each arm.

III.

Quick gushes from the summit dark the flash of fatal fires,
Yet upward charge those gallant men, whom Liberty inspires!

Like angered fiends they rush, they fight, they rally,
and they die—
The nightly mist has risen soft, the sunlight's in the
sky:
The sunlight gilds the shadowed Mount, and shows the
warry gleam
Of bayonets all deadly set, as in some horrid dream.
On, on they dash to where the foe, intrenched and
daring waits—
The very air is maddened now, and fraught with wing-
ing hates;
A struggle of contesting might is clashing in the clouds,
And Havoc grants its guerdon grim, but to the dead
no shrouds.
See! some assault, and some pursue, and some retire
dismayed:
It is the Rebel band that flies; the victors—Smith's
Brigade.

IV.

Oh! mighty spasm of human hearts; oh! wreck of
frenzied power;
The world is told through Glory's trump to mark the
deed and hour;
To cherish and exalt the brave, whose heroism outshines
In grand enduring memories, and unerasive lines!
Columbia's life is stronger grown: her faithless sons
recoil;
Their blood bedews the valley-heath, and clots the
mountain-soil;

A quiet briefly walks the wild, and noises deep and dread
Are hushed as are the lips that close the voices of the dead.
Pale smokes arise to upper air, to lave anon in tears
The grassy tufts, the glowing shades, that beautify the years;
But oh! the blaze of war revives, and still the deep-'ning groans
Of warrior-souls are murmuring above uncoffined bones.

GLIMPSES.

I.

The night was shadowing meadow and cottage,
    And homeward sauntered the herds,
As a child stood by a man in his dotage—
    Listening to his words.

II.

"The daylight's gone," quoth the withering mortal;
    "'Twill come again," said the child;
And soft and dreamily over the portal
    Fell moonbeams pure and mild.

* * * * * * * *

III.

Afar in the West loud storm-notes were rumbling,
    Clouds gathered 'twixt earth and sky;
The firmament—oh! 'twas awing, 'twas humbling
    To heart, and brain, and eye!

IV.

The bivouac-fagots were crackling to ashes—
  Eve was a truce to the foes;
'Thwart Heaven's dark arch flew the lightning's keen
    flashes,
  Burning the venoms that rose.

V.

Morn beamed; but alas! what murderous ruin!—
  Blood imbrued, humankind reeled;
Lost was the hour to rejoice, love or woo in—
  Torn was Amity's shield!

* * * * * * * *

VI.

O'er bone-strewn paths, where miscreant earthly glory
  Plucked vantage from pale slaughtered men,
Six horsemen hastened, in each breast a story—
  Dreadful to tell again.

VII.

Why rode they thus so mournful and so lonely,
  A weary, wan, and wasted band?
Two hundred souls they numbered erst, but only
  Six lived to tread the land!

VIII.

What sought they 'mong the butchered heaps and
    bloody—
  Blackening as the Past grew large?

Their chief—ay, he of hero-form and ruddy,
  Who led the daybreak charge.

IX.

They found him where the peril was the thickest,
  Where Carnage piled its highest mound;
Down sprang they quick, and those that were the
    quickest
  Bore him to safer ground.

X.

"My comrades," gasped he, "I am bleeding, dying—
  The East is as a rosy bride,
Yet smiles on horrors—see! the foe is flying—
  I'll to my sires," and died.

TO THE ANGEL, PEACE.

I.

Bright angel, Peace! sublimely thou may'st soar
Through summer-airs, that erst the fiend of War
Shook with hideous sounds that grieve no more.
    Thy white wings beam in happy purity—
    They ope—beneath them spreads security,
Confirmed amid the beauties of mountain-land and shore.

II.

Bright angel, Peace! thy smiles fell Discord's shades
Dispel, throughout my country's towns and glades:
Brave kinsmen sheathe antagonistic blades.
    As none thy true clemency accuses,
    'Tis but the obdurate heart refuses
A fallen brother's friendship, and deems that it degrades.

III.

Bright angel, Peace ! flee not away ; thy feet
In glory walk, thy hands in mercy meet,
To comfort all, and bless the rip'ning wheat.
    Oh ! ne'er let gentle, holy Charity
    With Freedom's sons be as a rarity—
Shine o'er us, and we'll love thee with love entrancing
    sweet.

EXULTATION.

JULY 4, 1865.

I.

Lift high our flag, by blood redeemed,
    With jubilant acclaim;
No grander epoch ever beamed,
    Than this, for Glory's name.
No brighter hour for Liberty
    Glowed since the world began—
For millions saved from anarchy
    Exalt the cause of Man!

II.

Let choruses from children rise,
    Responsive to the song
That angels chant, when destinies
    The joys of men prolong.
Let horrors blacken but the Past,
    The Present is of cheer;
Sweet Amity is ours—at last
    The smile supplants the tear.

III.

The world is glad, the realms serene
 Embody Nature's glee;
Our country's triumph pleases e'en
 The tyrants o'er the sea!
Green Erin lifts her fettered form,
 And Poland breathes a sigh
For Liberty, though battle's storm
 Has swept her plains and sky.

IV.

Lift high our flag, by blood redeemed,
 Dear countrymen and brave;
Full eighty years its folds have streamed,
 Ten thousand may they wave!
And fairest hands will fashion flowers
 In garlands, sweet and gay,
To beautify this flag of ours,
 So glorious to-day!

COUNSEL.

I.

My country is not *part*, but *all*
    Of its extent from sea to sea;
I will not, and I cannot call
    The North *alone* beloved by me.
I love the South, the East, the West,
    For they're my native land as well!
Each part full equal to the rest,
    And all as one in Freedom's swell.

II.

Is he a friend of humankind,
    Who agitates intestine feud?
Believe it not: the evil mind
    Is ever restless, not the good.
And countrymen, by war we've won
    The title to a common land;
Then who will dare take down the gun,
    And flame again Rebellion's brand?

III.

Recrimination curses yields,
  And 'tis a noble nation's pride
To build the cities, smooth the fields,
  That devastation wasted wide;
And hide the deep and bloody trace
  Of strife, with smiling homes and bowers;
In war we were a warrior-race,
  In peace be Love and Kindness ours!

PRAISE.

I.

Mine is a broad and bounteous land,
   Untrod by courtiers, kings, or slaves;
A freeman on its soil I stand,
   And oceans round it toss their waves
      In mystery,
      In majesty,
And chant within resounding caves
   The grandest tones of Freedom's song.
Its treasures are its heroes' graves,
   Its glory is its living throng;
Its flag—how loftily it braves
   The tyrants as it streams along!

II.

Mine is a green and varied land,
   Whose mountains, valleys, hills and plains
In peopled unity expand;
   Whose rivers course like mighty veins,
      Full rapidly,
      Full lucidly,
The offsprings of unnumbered rains,
   The inner paths of Power's career.
Midst all, with all, no chilling chains
   Bid Liberty to droop and fear;
Grim Monarchy such toys retains—
   They are not here—they are not here!

THE SHAMROCK AND LAUREL.

I.

There's a lofty love abounding
  In the emblem of a land;
There's a fellowship, confounding
  The evil mind and hand,
In the token of a nation,
  In the flow'ret of a race;
And a multiform oblation
    Is lifted by the grace
    And patriotism of millions—
To the hearthstones, homes and hamlets,
  Where gush the native fountains;
To the valleys, groves and streamlets,
  The cities and the mountains—
With a pride as high as Ilion's!

II.

As the Lily was the glory
  Of the olden flag of France,
As the Rose illumes the story
  Of Albion's advance—

In the Shamrock is communion
   Of all Irish faith and love,
And the Laurel crowns the union
   Of grandeurs interwove
   Round the temple of the Chainless.
To the Laurel fill libations,
   The cup with Shamrocks wreathing;
And before the monarch-nations
   Raise the symbol—breathing
   Equal Rights—to lordlings gainless!

III.

Interweave the lowly Shamrock,
   Freedom's Laurel to endow;
Ay! unite with Ireland's Shamrock
   Columbia's Laurel-bough—
For there's hope and help unchary
   Columbia's skies beneath,
And from ev'ry cliff and prairie
   To Erin's hills of heath,
   Salutations clear and cheerful
Resound across the ocean,
   And Celts, in might increasing,
With patriot emotion,
   Vow in their souls unceasing:
"WE'LL AVENGE THEE, MOTHER TEARFUL!"

THE RIGHTS OF MAN.

I.

When Misrule's night
　Wrapt lord and slave,
And gloomed the light
　That Glory gave,
Above the West
　Burst forth a sign—
To lords unblest,
　To slaves divine—
And thus the glorious symbol ran:
"To all belong the Rights of Man!"

II.

The tyrant frowned,
　The courtier threw
His gauntlet, bound
　With favors new;
And as it fell,
　Thus challenged he
The world, whose spell
　Was Liberty:
"The power of Kings shall crush and ban
Who dare uphold the Rights of Man!"

III.

Ten thousand swords,
   In patriot hands,
Gleamed round the words
   That woke all lands
With fervent hope,
   And brave desire,
Misrule to cope
   With, and acquire
In halls of State, and Battle's van,
The vindicated Rights of Man.

IV.

And since that hour,
   When Tyranny
Reeled 'neath the power
   Of Liberty,
The exiled found
   A refuge bright—
A vantage-ground
   To Wrong requite,
And strike at tyrants, as they can,
With swords that flash the Rights of Man.

THOMAS FRANCIS MEAGHER.

Died July 1, 1867.

I.

And is the patriot, Meagher, dead?
   Who in his youthful glory rose,
A champion of his race, and led
   His country 'gainst her foes.
Who prized the sword 'bove "moral force,"
   When Tyranny to dotage ran,
And waked in tyrants a remorse
   For slavery in man.

II.

And is the orator, Meagher, dead?
   Whose silver voice rang to the skies,
And men and angels 'raptured said:
   "This man's divinely wise!"
His wit was of a golden glee,
   His pathos flowed, a summer-stream,
And, oh! his eloquence was free
   When Ireland was the theme!

III.

And is the soldier, Meagher, dead?
  And lost his burning, martial word?
Weep, weep, O comrades, mourning shed
  For "Meagher of the Sword!"
Ye saw him grasp proud Freedom's shield,
  Ye saw him flash along the war;
He would not blanch, he would not yield
  From out the flag a star!

IV.

Weep, weep, O Erin, for thy son!
  Weep, weep, Columbia, he was thine:
His deeds were ever nobly done,
  His fame shall live and shine.
The patriot of a brave revolt,
  The orator of heavenly breath,
The soldier of the thunderbolt,
  Are dead in Meagher's death!

THE MEMORY OF THE BRAVE.

I.

The Genius of each age records
    Heroic, bright, and noble deeds,
'Midst clash of musketry and swords,
    'Midst tramp of foemen and of steeds.
O'er Battle's horrid scene of woes,
    Where flashes high the crimsoned glaive,
The heart a coronal bestows
    To the Memory of the Brave.

II.

Thermopylæ and Marathon
    Shine grand as sunlight on the seas;
And vivify those heroes gone—
    Leonidas, Miltiades.
The glories of the Grecian State—
    Rome's prowess on the land and wave—
Awake the chords of praise elate
    To the Memory of the Brave.

III.

Europa's heather-vales attest
    The valor of Caucasian blood:
Unawed by tyrant-power unblest,
    The Knights of Freedom stoutly stood.
Ay, many fought in fierce crusade,
    And many piled the hallowed grave—
Let not polluted tongues upbraid
    The darling Mem'ry of the Brave.

IV.

Upon the blooming Western Land
    The flash of warry lightnings came;
Victory smiled on Freedom's band,
    And Tyranny crouched low in shame.
Where rest the valiant—spirit-free—
    Oblivion's tide shall never lave;
For heart-enshrined will ever be
    The Mem'ry of the faithful Brave.

V.

Let nations honor, long and well,
    The noble hearts that pine and bleed
On battle-ground, in martyr-cell,
    And plant 'midst horrors Freedom's seed.
Oh, green in Recollection's maze
    Be ev'ry patriot hero's grave:
Posterity its voice will raise
    And bless the Mem'ry of the Brave!

IV.

NATURE AND ART.

I.

1.

I TREAD dear Nature's glowing solitude,
  And around me bright inspiration beams,
Engendering fancies.   Benignly rude
  It is: green brakes, and dales, and moss-bound
      streams,
Unused to mortal trespass, blossom-strewed,
  A welcome give to light and happy dreams.

2.

Gray mountains, robust, craggy, and sublime,
  Cleave lightsome clouds, and whiten far above;
As lofty as in Earth's created prime,
  Unmoved by blasts that devastate the grove.

III.

The sky in softest tint and grace appears,
  High o'er the glories of the pristine realm;
Celestial brightness ev'ry space endears,
  As flow'rets smile 'neath shades of oak and elm.

IV.

Uprise the tinctured and complacent hills,
  To guard the beauties of the vales below;
And adown their gorges the sweet-toned rills
  In crystalline purity dash and flow.

V.

The creatures of the woods, to freedom born,
  Around their native wild unfrightened roam;
Man dwells apart, and the hunter's horn
  Thrills not the caverns of their forest-home.

VI.

Down to the haunts of flowers my vision strays,
  And verdant depths ecstatic thoughts allure;
My heart throbs light, and gives to God fond praise
  For all the bloom, so sunny-hued and pure.

VII.

Cliff, plain and river, slope and grassy glade,
  Combine their charms, and verify my dreams
Of peace and bliss, as foams the swift cascade
  O'er rocks, through meadow-land, with constant gleam.

VIII.

Yes! here in grand old Nature's wide-spread wild,
   I listen to the strains that heavenward rise,
And muse, and wish myself as undefiled
   As this lone scene, of worldly things unwise!

II.

I.

I view thy chiseled piles, O gracious Art,
   Lavish with arches, towers, and shining spires;
And gaze on palace, mansion-house and mart,
   Reared for man's solace, and his great desires.

II.

Proud homes appear, of timber and of stone,
   And ornaments adorn, of scarce design:
The peasant's cottage, modest and alone,
   A contrast gives, as o'er it creeps the vine.

III.

Genius here its mighty labor spreads—
   Glorious the outline, and the inner space—
Painting a spirit-influence ever sheds,
   And Sculpture lends to all a noble grace.

IV.

Oh! would that Happiness ungrieved could dwell
   Where beauteous Art holds temporary reign—
Contention's clouds forever to dispel,
   And Charity, Hope, Love and Truth retain.

v.

Trim work of man—flattering to his pride!
 I'd fain desert your cold, unconscious walls,
And in Nature's haunts, luxuriant and wide,
 Dream 'mong forest-shades, hills, and waterfalls!

SOCIETY'S SEA.

I.

THERE arose on the moody breeze of Night
    A voice from Society's Sea;
And I reviewed anon a luring light,
That lit up a wave of blemishless white,
    But I said, "It is not for me."

II.

"It is not for me," I said, as I gazed
    Wide over the varying flood;
"For my brain's ablaze, and my heart's amazed,
To behold sweet Virtue buffeted, dazed,
    And Evil thus conquering Good."

III.

A maidenly form on the stainless wave
    Beamed o'er it in Purity's sheen;
'Twas mystic, divine, 'twas sight for the brave,
And she seemed to surmount Sin and the grave,
    Like Mary, the Cherubim-Queen.

IV.

She saw the ripples of Folly afar,
  Beyond them a deepening waste,
Unlit by a ray, ungemmed by a star,
And—dupes that children of Innocence are—
  Sought in her soul some germ disgraced.

V.

Then a smiling fiend at her side thus spoke,
  Persuasive as a foe of Heaven—
"What fear'st thou, angel? yon gloom is the cloak
That veils a beautiful realm, where the yoke
  Of exquisite passion is riven!"

VI.

An ebony wave upheaved at their feet—
  She stept from the pure to the vile:
Oh! swift are the lurements of glozing Deceit,
And my heart grew sad that a soul so sweet
  Society thus should defile.

VII.

Not lost! not lost! for a youth o'er the wave,
  As Virtue's knight-errant, pursued—
Pursued to the bounds of Chastity's grave,
And the demon's front full merciless clave,
  With the sword defensive of Good!

VIII.

And a halo from the morning of grace
  Shone round the savior and the saved;
And the shadows died from her form and face—
For she stood again in her virginal place,
  'Mong the Beautiful, undepraved!

A VISION.

I.

In a nook of a house where join many eaves,
    And cozy security sanctifies rest,
A dreamer bright thoughts into melody weaves,
    And sings out his soul from the warmth of his breast.

II.

Apart from the turbulent world of the Real,
    Pure dreams of the Beautiful soothingly rise,
And an angel-form opes the shrine of Ideal,
    With the glory of Heaven enriching her eyes.

III.

A vision uplooms amidst petulant clouds,
    That seemingly battle, its glare to o'ershade:
Eternity's semblance appears, and the crowds
    Of the silent spirit-world glitter and fade.

IV.

The souls that have prayed, and the souls that have fought,
    Outshine in their happiness, shrink in their woe;
O'er-thronging the realms of the universe Thought—
    The saints on the hills, and the demons below.

V.

Aloft in the zenith the light of the Good,
    Enwreathed with the splendors of seraphic wings,
Delights, as the sun in its summer-tide mood,
    And blesses the toilers as well as the kings!

VI.

Ay! th' angels, that stand and repose on the hills,
    All equal and blissful exult in its beams;
And the spirits of doom, 'midst shadows and ills,
    Upgaze with a longing, that sorrowful seems.

VII.

It departs, that vision of torment and weal,
    Like a vapor devoured by the radiant East,
When Night and its phantoms to nothingness steal,
    And the glow of the world is by Heaven increased.

TO TRAGEDY.

A SONNET.

HAIL! sublime offspring of the mimic Muse,
As from her cloud-wrapt throne thy powers infuse
Earth's Genius with brain-ennobling fires;
Whereby depicted are men's passions, ires,
And what their souls contain, that all may see
Profound existence in epitome!
Thy sphere is where the dim and narrow stage
Unfolds a massive world. Thy Love and Rage
Are there revealed, as in Time's wider scene
They burn, transpire; racking the jeweled queen
And her subject-slave with passionate power
Alike, though placed distinct, as speeds the hour—
The circumstantial hour of human life,
In which, O Tragedy, Love rules with Rage and Strife!

THE OUTCAST'S GRAVE.

I.

APART from the rest, in the dark clod alone,
With noxious weeds and rank herbage o'ergrown,
  Is seen the outcast's grave.
There's not e'en a slab or purchaseless stone,
Save the pebbly ones, o'er the dust unknown,
  That human tears ne'er lave.

II.

Oh, why reposes this remnant of dust
Companionless, far from the lauded just,
  In such a dreary grave?
"She Virtue scorned," say those mortals whose trust
Seems holy, " her life was darkened with lust,
  And sank where demons rave!"

III.

Charity! how true is the baleful tale
Of this worthless earth in its darksome jail,
  That Pity's tear doth crave?
It erst had a spirit, like those who rail,
And heart of love, and cheeks of bloom, now pale—
  Dead in the outcast's grave!

IV.

Why place it lonely here, why is't not found
Among the rest, with white mausoleums crowned,
    Within a cherished grave?
Though Sin, forsooth, has piled the outcast's mound,
Can native earth pollute its native ground,
    Has Sin no other slave?

V.

There's interest here: a vision gaunt appears,
As meditation drifts adown the years,
    On Time's uncertain wave.
Humanity! she shrinks not at your jeers,
She's dead—the clouds but mourn, and drop their tears
    Upon the outcast's grave!

WEALTH NO MERIT.

I.

Though philosophers curb emotions,
   Divines anath'matize Pride,
Humanity still has its notions,
   As the sea its changing tide;
And the glitter of Wealth lures about it
   The weakest, the fairest, ay, those
Who'd banish the cynic who'd flout it,
   And scoff at its tinseled woes!

II.

See the genius, with garments tattered,
   Grasping his manuscript-roll,
In his nook, by the wild winds battered—
   Who comforts his mighty soul?
Not the simpering levees that gather
   In false, luxurious ease;
Not the lovers of fashion—but rather
   The unrecognized of these!

III.

Humanity! rise, as you rally
  From Pride's insidious snares;
Full worthy, as flowers of the valley
  That sweeten the mountain airs!
Let fools all follies inherit,
  And Intellect sovereign be;
Then none will be great without merit,
  Then Talent and Truth shall be free!

CHANGES.

I.

How meek the soul becomes,
   When chill misfortune sears:
Devouring e'en the crumbs
   It loathed in former years.
How suppliant it seems,
   So haughty in the Past!
Are Wealth and Glory dreams,
   That they so briefly last?

II.

The beggar doffs his hood
   To men of nobler mien,
Though purer be his blood
   Than flows through king or queen.
The monarch forfeits rule,
   And, high in sovereign-place,
Above a crimson pool,
   The beggar sways his race!

III.

Then who will dare be proud—
  For what is mortal pride?
At noon, a silken shroud,
  At eve, a garb decried!
The glee of summer-hours
  Precedes a winter-grief;
And where bloomed freshest flowers
  Appears a shrivel'd leaf!

MORALITY.

I.

The righteous mandate of the Good,
    And Virtue's handmaid true—
Erect and beautiful it stood,
    As humankind the better grew.

II.

In places where God's might is taught,
    Where truths spread far and wide,
'Tis there it always should be sought,
    And there it always should abide.

III.

At home, around the fireside-hearth,
    In beauty let it reign;
And those who wish for right on earth
    Should strive its purpose to sustain.

IV.

'Mid social circles, where unite
    The young, of manners gay,
This theme should be the shining light
    To guide grave Duty on its way.

REMEMBER DEATH.

I.

REMEMBER, O Humanity!
   The end of earthly life;
Let not the heart with vanity
   Be filled, nor sin grow rife
Within the deathless soul.
God's holy name extol—
          Remember Death!

II.

Ye rulers, and ye modest poor,
   Shackled with worldly cares,
Keep, keep your many spirits pure,
   By soul-repentant prayers!
Oh! walk the brightened way,
For Earth is as a day—
          Remember Death!

III.

Solemn the hour—Eternity!
  By sacred words defined;
The perils of Death's shadowy sea—
  Absorbing to the mind.
Grand Christian truths remain:
May all God's blessings gain—
        Remember Death!

LINES TO A BRILLIANT STAR.

I.

Shine on, shine on, O Star,
   High in the crown of Night;
May naught thy glory mar,
   Though hidden oft from sight.

II.

Thou glitt'rest for mortals
   In this their home below—
Brightening Heaven's portals,
   So constant to bestow.

III.

Clouds many times o'ercast
   Thy cheerful, sparkling face;
But when anon they've passed,
   Thou beam'st in all thy grace.

IV.

Shine on, shine on, O Star,
   With others of thy kind;
And from Night's crown afar,
   Flash pleasures to the mind.

AN IMPRESSION.

I.

I sat in the moonlight, and read of the " Raven "—
    The " Raven " of Poe's strange genius born ;
And its words seemed by weird handicraft graven,
    From the heart of a wretched man torn.
I thought—and my thoughts were not critical—craven—
    What miseries blast the forlorn !

II.

'Twas night in the poem, 'twas night o'er the city,
    Dreary the one, the other full bright,
And there rose in my soul an impulse of pity,
    As the shadows evaded the light !
Oh ! why was man made so gifted and witty,
    Yet doomed to Passion's grim blight ?

III.

A sympathy, true as the blest love of Nature,
  Burning in grand, poetical souls,
Wrought brotherhood in my heart for the creature,
  Whose chilly dirge high Memory tolls;
Whose works will remain a proud nomenclature,
  While merit enlightens the scrolls!

IV.

I went to my rest, and the moonlight was streaming
  As lucid and pale as before;
And images of my fancy, sad-seeming,
  Flitted ghost-like over the floor—
Wild, wild were my dreams, for that night I was dreaming
  Of shapes that shrieked " Nevermore!"

STANZAS.

I.

Enshrined in Fancy's bowers,
Bloom bright and tender flowers,
O'er which the sky oft lowers,
   And falls the chilly rain;
Of beauty, thought-designed,
Of perfume, soul-refined,
Smile lilies of the mind,
   Blush roses of the brain.

II.

Ah! Melancholy, thou
Com'st o'er my musings now,
And specters 'thwart the brow
   Of Fancy throng amain;
And dimming with the light
That dazzled Reason's sight,
Expire in mental night
   The bright bloom of the brain.

THE NEW YEAR.

I.

Full many years have come and gone,
  Since Order out of Chaos came;
Still roll the years sublimely on,
  Through light and darkness, shade and flame.

II.

Hope fondles to her heart the New,
  And Memory enshrines the Old;
'Twas youthful, hopeful, glowing too,
  Till griefs o'erflecked its locks of gold.

III.

The cottage and the palace beam,
  And wars are 'feebled 'midst the joy
That laughs the New Year in, and seem
  Too unimpassioned to destroy!

IV.

Methinks in ev'ry breast there beats
  A universal throb of cheer;
And ev'ry voice the prayer repeats:
  "O God, be this a glad New Year!"

AMBITION.

Ambition 'woke, and o'er his head
    There glittered high a star;
"I'll to yon light," Ambition said,
    "Though blood and deluge bar!"
He flew to gain the dazzling world
    That shone in air afar;
But fitful winds him backward hurled,
    And fought with force of war.
He rose, all dangers downward trod,
    And boldly reached the star;
But, ah! it seemed a diresome clod,
    As Earth's attainments are!
A brighter orb its glory shed,
"I'll to it fly!" Ambition said.

NOTES.

[1] Written in 1868.

[2] THE PALISADES comprise a high, precipitous range of rocks, commencing opposite Manhattan Island (on which the City of New York stands), and extending along the western shore of the Hudson River, a distance of twenty miles.

[3] THE HIGHLANDS are a romantic group of hills, sloping steeply among the windings of the Hudson, and rearing their noble forms northward of "Tappan Bay."

[4] THE BATTLE OF LOOKOUT MOUNTAIN, otherwise "Wauhatchie." took place October 28, 1863, between the Confederate and Federal troops, commanded respectively by Gen'ls Longstreet and Hooker. The following extract from Major-General Hooker's Report, dated November 6, 1863, chronicles the splendid charge of "Smith's Brigade" (Federal), commanded by Col. Orlan Smith, of the 73d Ohio Volunteers, up the mountain:—

"This skeleton but brave brigade charged up the mountain, almost inaccessible by daylight, under a heavy fire, without returning it, and drove three times their number from behind the hastily thrown-up intrenchments; capturing prisoners, and scattering the enemy in all directions. No troops ever rendered more brilliant service."

www.ingramcontent.com/pod-product-compliance
Lightning Source LLC
Chambersburg PA
CBHW022126160426
43197CB00009B/1163